The Illustrated BESTIARY

Guidance and Rituals from 36 Inspiring Animals

MAIA TOLL

Illustrations by Kate O'Hara

Storey Publishing

The mission of Storey Publishing is to serve our customers by
publishing practical information that encourages
personal independence in harmony with the environment.

Edited by Liz Bevilacqua

Art direction and book design by Jessica Armstrong

Text production by Erin Dawson

Illustrations by © Kate O'Hara, except © Jason Winter/shutterstock.com, 13 and throughout

Author photo by © Emily Nichols Photography

Text © 2019 by Maia Toll

Storey books are available at special discounts when purchased in bulk for premiums and sales promotions as
well as for fund-raising or educational use. Special editions or book excerpts can also be created to specifica-
tion. For details, please call 800-827-8673, or send an email to sales@storey.com.

Storey Publishing
210 MASS MoCA Way
North Adams, MA 01247
storey.com

Printed in China through Asia Pacific Offset
10   9   8   7   6   5   4   3   2

Library of Congress Cataloging-in-Publication Data on file

This publication is intended to provide educational information on the covered subject.
It is not intended to take the place of personalized medical counseling, diagnosis, and treatment
from a trained health professional.

To the four-leggeds and the winged ones
and those who swim the sea: thank you for
remembering what we have forgotten . . .

And to Andrew and the beasts for
navigating this luscious life beside me.

CONTENTS

The Bestiary

Every creature of the world
is a book or picture, and also
a mirror for ourselves.

— ALAIN DE LILLE, TWELFTH CENTURY
(from *Holy Dogs and Asses: Animals in the
Christian Tradition* by Laura Hobgood-Oster)

We are, indeed, unique primates,
we humans, but we're simply not as
different from the rest of the animal
kingdom as we used to think.

— JANE GOODALL

Preface

The air smelled of apples and woodsmoke and the warm, strawlike scent of freshly cut corn. Although it seemed impossible to get lost with a rural road on one side and a river on the other, as I crouched and crunched through the autumn leaves a small part of me worried that I wouldn't be able to find my way back.

But something held me in its thrall, tugging me deeper into the woods that lined my friend's freshly shorn fields. I crossed a small clearing almost on my hands and knees . . . and then, I can't say why exactly, felt I'd gone too far. Turning around slowly, chills went up my spine. Rising out of the ground (which I could have sworn I'd just crawled over) were five bone-white tines.

Despite years of studying religion and spirituality, this gathering, which had sent me wandering into the woods, was my first encounter with a medicine woman. Two medicine women, actually. Both were trained in the old ways and had come to lead a land-blessing on a friend's farm. Just ten minutes before, thirty of us had stood around the campfire, listening to these women speak about our relationship to the land and the cycle of the seasons. Then they'd sent us out to find something we could offer as a gift — a metaphor for our blessings — such as a stone to signify strength or the empty curl of a cocoon to symbolize regeneration.

As I set off around the edge of the field to find my gift, some instinct pulled me into the woods . . . and ten minutes later I walked out with a deer antler.

Never has the magic of the world felt as close as it did in those moments when the spirit of Deer seemed to whisper: *It's time to walk a new path.*

Whether it's time to walk a new path or refresh your commitment to an old one, this Bestiary is a doorway to the magic inherent in the wild world in which we live. May it reconnect you with a sense of mystery that ignites your spirit, reminding you that you, too, are part of a greater whole.

Maia

Introduction

Don Antonio sat at the back of the boat making minute movements with his fingers and chuckling to himself. The Amazon River was broad and sluggish, and we were drifting only slightly faster than the mesmerizing motion of the shaman's fingers. He caught me watching and nodded toward the jungle. Not for the first time, I scanned the treeline, baffled.

It was a few days before I realized he was imitating the sloths, *perezoso* in Spanish. They hung from branches high in the canopy, the moss growing off their backs blending them seamlessly with the foliage. Sloths do move, but you'll need a huge dose of patience to see it. Don Antonio imitated their slow-motion movement, amusing himself for hours as we toured the river.

Teaching beside a real-deal shaman was eye-opening in none of the ways I expected. Sure, there were ceremonies filled with strange scents and mysterious chanting, but the real lessons were the quiet ones. Witnessing how Don Antonio moved through the world – reverent and humble, curious and laughing – was a gift in itself.

But the deepest understandings came when we connected, through sign language and broken English, about his childhood. His uncle was the village shaman and Don Antonio his chosen apprentice. To be clear: this was not a glamorous post – it was a lonely one. At a very young age, Don Antonio spent months by himself seeing his cousins only when they brought food into the jungle for him.

Listening to the stories of this young boy, sequestered in solitude, turning to the animals and plants for solace, echoed the intense loneliness I felt when I lived in Ireland, apprenticed to a medicine woman. Far from friends and family, I, like Don Antonio, began to turn toward nonhuman companionship. I played my wooden flute for the swans on the river or the cows in the field; I turned to the Hawthorn tree for sympathy; I let the ravens bolster me with their harsh cries. I became one strand, one life force among many, and part of the larger tapestry of existence.

The deep knowledge that I was woven-in and integral cured some nameless longing that had haunted me since childhood. Something in me calmed and became still.

This is the magic earth medicine — the medicine of the plants and animals, the stones and sky. It connects us not only to the world around us but also back to ourselves and our sense of groundedness, inner-knowing, and deep wisdom. It reminds us we are never alone.

Working with animal medicine is about opening your mind and heart to the energies animals hold in the world and then gently asking what they have to teach you. While the animals you find in this book may not live near you, their energy is part of the web of which you too are a part. We share this world with so many creatures, each holding a place not only in the physical world but also in the ecosystem of spirit.

When we talk about habitat loss and animal extinction, I can't help but wonder what energies the world will lose when a particular species passes from this earth. If they are gone in physical form, will we remember the farsightedness of Eagle and the deep understanding of Dolphin?

We humans are part of this tapestry as well. Sometimes we are threads, sometimes weavers, and sometimes, like the Greek fates, it is we who cut the threads, our actions rippling across the lives of many species. We live in a complex world where all things are intertwined in the loom of creation. When we understand this, we begin to know what the shaman knows: that to become whole and healed you must remember what you have forgotten — that we humans are a thread in the larger web of creation.

The Bestiary Watch List

Due to changes in climate, deforestation, and loss of ecosystem, many animals are struggling to survive. To increase awareness, this icon marks the most vulnerable species in this book.

HEARING SPIRIT'S SONG

I think of the song of the spirit as a kind of *second song,* a counterpoint and harmony existing parallel to what our cognitive mind understands. While animals are physical beings they are also spirits and guides. Their second song connects us to necessary parts of our own psyche.

How do you hear an animal's second song? It begins with simply tuning in to the world around you. Once, when I was out on a walk with friends, a peregrine falcon flew ten feet in front of our faces. My friends were engrossed in conversation and neither of them noticed.

What animals are around you? Who is not simply crossing your path but sparking your imagination, or trying to get your attention? Sometimes an animal will seep into your subconscious, like the way Horse came to me over and over again as a child. When you begin seeing an animal in daydreams and nighttime dreams, in meditation, and on shamanic journeys, it's time to take note.

Sometimes you'll find clues in the physical world. You might find feathers or see photographs or notice an animal on the jersey of your favorite basketball team. You can also use the cards that come with this book to ask yourself: *Who wants to guide me right now? Who has a lesson for me today?*

HOW TO USE THIS BOOK

This book is meant to inspire you to feel into the energy of different animals with rituals and reflections to help you dive deeper and connect more fully. You can draw a card from the deck to guide your day, open the book to a random page and see who wants to speak with you, or read the book cover-to-cover to familiarize yourself with all the animals here. If you want to connect more deeply to an animal's medicine, try this:

BE THE ANIMAL

There's an ancient tradition of slipping into the skin of an animal to see how it feels to be that animal, to look at the world through the eyes of a deer or a duck or a wolf. You don't need to literally wear animal skin to do this. Instead, watch a few videos to see how an animal moves and reacts. Then find a comfortable (and private!) place to close your eyes and picture the animal. Breathe as though your breath is the animal's breath. Allow the feeling of the animal to come into your body. Try moving like your animal. *How would this animal feel? What would it be like to see through its eyes?* Ask yourself: *What can I learn from this experience?*

INVITE THE ANIMAL INTO YOUR DREAMTIME

Before sleep, and after the lights are out, sit on the side of the bed with your feet flat on the floor. Sit up tall, allowing your body to be a conduit between the earth and sky. Breathe here, feeling your skin, quieting your thoughts. Picture your mind like a pond or a watering hole. Invite any animals who have a message to come visit this pond during dreamtime.

Keep a journal by your bed so you can make notes of any nocturnal visitors.

FREE WRITE

Free writing is a way to tap into the collective unconscious. You'll need a pen and paper as well as a timer.

- Set the timer for 10 minutes.
- Start by drawing a Bestiary card, then ask: *What message do you have for me?*
- Begin writing and don't stop until the timer goes off. The idea is to continue writing even when you have no idea what words will come next! This will help you move beyond your conscious thoughts and into the subconscious realm. The first few minutes are often filled with nonsense. Don't worry — just keep writing. You need to get beyond the protective barrier of your thinking mind to let in messages from your subconscious.

The animals have much to teach and much to share when you open your spirit ears to hear them. May the spirit of the animals inspire you to gather the medicine you need to heal yourself, your family, your community, and our shared world.

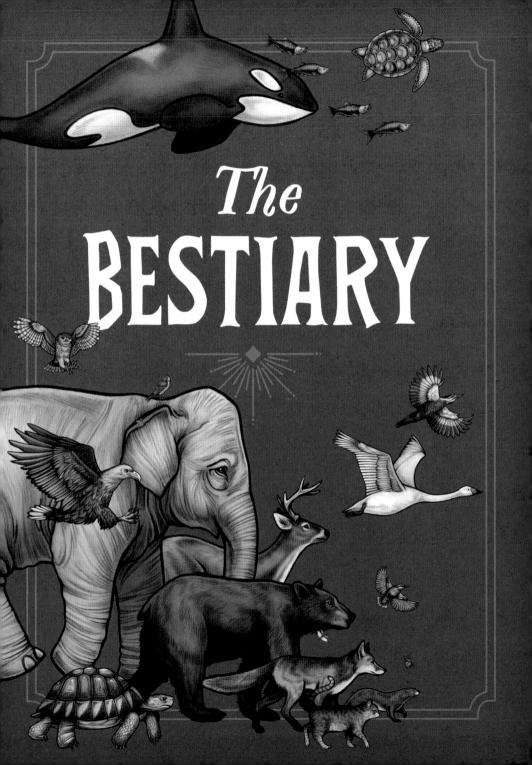

The
BESTIARY

Pause, Assess, Act

WHITE-TAILED DEER

Odocoileus virginianus

Step delicately and truly, Deer advises, *trust your intention, intuition, and your ability to move decisively.* The first step in taking decisive action is to pause and get the lay of the land. Never one for snap decisions, Deer freezes, feeling into each new situation, reaching out with all her senses, then steps gracefully and surely into whatever's next. She'll gift you with self-confidence, especially as you move through life's cyclical changes — those times when one season of your life is ending and another is about to begin. Trust Deer's medicine to help you make a definitive decision and then step into it with grace.

MAP YOUR MOOD

Unlike most other animals, Deer's medicine is often specific to the age and gender of the deer:

Fawn represents virginal innocence.
Doe represents gentle mothering.
Buck represents robust and wild virility.

This triad mirrors the internal energies within each of us. At various points in our lives our energy will align more with one than the others. Acknowledging where we're at shows us how our creative energy is flowing.

Which face of Deer are you currently wearing?
Are you feeling innocent and new? Protective
and nurturing? Robust and virile?

What's the energy of this season of your life?

Make a mood board to honor the aspects of Deer you're currently expressing. You can do this the old-fashioned way by collecting images and tacking them on a board, or with an online collage or mood board application.

···· *Reflection* ····

THE POWER OF THE PIVOT

While Deer is a prey animal, swift and wily, she is far from helpless.
Deer is known for duplicity, deceiving hunters into a false chase.
Deer enters dense underbrush then gracefully and quickly pivots,
running off in a different direction.

*How can you, like Deer,
use your strengths and
your smarts to change
the balance of power?*

*What change of course will
cause an unexpected result?*

*Can you pivot when
things are looking
overwhelming or hopeless?*

*Step out of the history that is holding you back.
Step into the new story you are willing to create.*

Oprah Winfrey

21

RED SALMON

Oncorhynchus nerka

Quit griping and get going! quips Salmon. And she should know: Salmon swims thousands of miles, undaunted by eagles, bears, and waterfalls. And just when she's at her weakest and most exhausted, her route turns mostly upstream. This isn't an accident. Salmon didn't get lost or find herself turned around. On the contrary, Salmon is one of the finest navigators to swim the Seven Seas; she can always find her way home. Salmon will help you plumb the depths of your own unconscious to discover the energy and determination to get to your soul's destination. Call on Salmon to help you navigate life with determination, meaning, and purpose.

····Ritual····
REVIVING RECIPROCITY

Salmon travels thousands of miles, first across oceans and then upstream, steering by starlight and the subtle pull of magnetic fields to reach the hatching grounds where she was born. Fraught with danger, first in the oceans' depths where Salmon is food for sharks, seals, and humans, and then on the river where she dodges eagles and bears, Salmon makes her way home.

This journey is heroic; the final stages more so. Salmon — now accustomed to a seafood diet from years of ocean living — finds no food as she moves up the freshwater river. Her skin begins to dissolve. But determined Salmon will complete her journey, spawning where she was hatched. Most likely, Salmon will die after laying her eggs. Her body will then leach phosphorus into the water, a necessary nutrient for young salmon, beginning the cycle again.

Salmon teaches that you must give back to the river and the land which gave you life. For the next week, make daily gifts to the land or a river if you have one nearby. Maybe it's egg shells (full of calcium) or seeds sprinkled for the birds. Maybe you'll offer mulch to your garden. Give back and in giving back remember what it's like to be part of the cycle of exchange.

····· *Reflection* ·····
WATERY WISDOM

In Ireland they tell a tale in which a very ordinary salmon eats nine hazelnuts that had fallen into the Well of Wisdom. After a dunk in the well, those hazelnuts contained all the knowledge in the world. After ingesting this rich feast, the salmon was not so ordinary any more.

The Salmon of Knowledge is the ultimate catch, the big kahuna. Spiritually, this is what we're all fishing for.

Why do you think the ancient Irish connected
Salmon with the potential to become wise?

Potential for wisdom is not the same as having it:
how can you grow into your own wisdom?

And what can Salmon teach you
about this process?

Some of the native tribes in North America associate salmon with reincarnation and the cycles of renewal.

Align Your Inner Compass
COMMON RAVEN

Corvus corax

Deep in Raven's heart is an ancient secret, a memory as tattered as his feathers are after harrying hawks. Few alive remember that Raven used to be as white as freshly fallen snow. Having himself been through the subtle shifting of transformation and rebirth, Raven knows that the world is often not quite what it seems. In the blink of an eye, light becomes shadow and shadow shifts to light. And so Raven is not one for rules or morality. Raven knows that sometimes the only way to course-correct is to step out of the boxes culture creates and align instead with your inner compass. *What's the highest good?* asks this winged trickster, *and what are you willing to sacrifice to bring it into the light?*

Ritual

STEPPING INTO SOVEREIGNTY

Many a god and goddess have cloaked themselves in Raven feathers, shifting form to fly over battlefields, protecting chosen warriors and ushering the dead to the afterlife.

Raven was but one form of the Goddess Morrigan, who the Celts both honored and feared. While the Morrigan in her raven cloak was well known as Queen of the War, she had another face: the face of sovereignty.

Sovereignty is an ancient concept which ties the land to its people and the people to their land. Sovereignty in its purest form is not about ownership; it's about relationship.

In modern days, our primary relationships are often with other people. *But what if your primary relationship was with yourself and, from a place of self-sovereignty, with the land?*

Find a place to sit quietly outdoors. And remember, this is not about ownership, it's about relationship. You do not need to own the land on which you are sitting! Place both hands over your heart and breathe, finding your center. When you feel quiet in yourself, move your hands to lie flat on the earth. Breathe here. Allow yourself to feel and believe you are in relationship, a circle of give and take, a cycle of sovereignty.

NOTICING NUANCE

In the tales of people native to the Pacific Northwest, Raven stole the sun. *Bad Raven!* you might think. But life is rarely so cut-and-dry:

In time's beginning, the world lived in darkness. In this swirling and never-ending night lived Raven. Raven's feathers were as white as the stars that did not yet shine, and his heart was as fiery as the absent sun. Raven fell in love with Eagle's daughter and, as often happens during courtship, was invited to Eagle's home.

When Raven entered Eagle's aerie, he was startled to find a massive globe of fire warming Eagle's hearth. This fiery sphere was enough to light not just the aerie but the whole benighted world. Raven knew what he had to do and the love it would cost. But the world was dark and filled with suffering, so Raven grabbed that fiery globe and soared up Eagle's chimney. Raven flew higher and higher, his bright white wings now covered in chimney soot.

With Eagle in chase, Raven hurled the fiery sphere as hard and high as he possibly could. Eagle screeched in fury as the Sun flew out of his reach and settled, sighing, into its home in the sky. To this day, Raven's wings remain dark as the night that existed before he stole the sun.

Is there a situation or person you are seeing as fixed, but might actually be as mutable as Raven's feathers?

Digest Your Past
MONARCH BUTTERFLY

Danaus plexippus

Before Butterfly can earn her wings, she turns inward, examining all she has been, digesting the pieces of her own past. This is quiet work, womb work, so she shuts herself away from the world to begin the deconstruction. As she performs the rites of unmaking, she sacrifices every bit of self on the altar of transformation. Finally, her body reduced to a soup of cells, Butterfly checks her blueprint, pulling proteins into wings, preparing, finally, for flight. If Monarch Butterfly appears in your life, it's time to begin the shedding, digesting your past, and doing the work that prepares you for flight.

····· *Ritual* ·····

WRITE YOUR PERSONAL MANIFESTO

Butterfly goes into her chrysalis with only the barest idea of who she will become when she emerges. This "idea" is called an *imaginal disc*, a group of cells holding the pattern of the parts she will need to create in order to take flight.

You, too, have metaphoric imaginal discs, patterns embedded deep in your psyche that help you know who you are. You can follow these patterns to rebuild yourself during transitions.

Let's pull these patterns to the surface so you can see them and begin to understand the essence of your own being.

Chrysalis or Cocoon

When moth larvae are ready to grow wings, they spin a silk shell called a cocoon.

When a butterfly larva (a caterpillar) is ready to transform and take flight, it first becomes a chrysalis: a hard, hanging teardrop of self. The chrysalis is the butterfly!

- Set a timer for 10 minutes and use the time to write a personal manifesto.
- Start with the phrase "I am" or "I honor" or "This is what is most important to me."
- When you're done writing, underline 3 to 5 of the most important sentences, crafting them into a personal manifesto that you can refer to when you feel like cellular soup with no clue how to re-emerge.

Reflection
PREPARING FOR CHANGE

It isn't news that Butterfly begins life as a caterpillar. But how does this most land-bound of creatures grow wings and take flight? She digests herself, literally.

When Caterpillar is ready to transform, she begins munching leaves at an alarming rate, stoking her energy and creative fires in a pre-transition feeding frenzy. When she is sated, Butterfly creates a hard exoskeleton to protect herself as she begins the messy work of transformation.

Once inside her chrysalis, Butterfly begins eating herself, digesting and assimilating every bit of her being, until she becomes cellular soup. This soup contains the building blocks of her future form. After Butterfly has dissolved her past, she begins the process of becoming, creating wings to gift herself with flight. This process is a metaphoric map for stepping consciously into changes in your own life:

- Nourish your body and spirit
- Release what no longer serves
- Take time and space alone
- Grow new wings

Think back to your largest life transition (perhaps having a child, moving to a new house, going through a divorce) and see how you worked through all the stages of transformation. How can you traverse your next change with grace?

Evolve into Your Next Becoming

SPRING PEEPER

Pseudacris crucifer

Big name, small frog. So small, in fact, you may think you don't know this critter at all. But if you've cracked a window on an early spring evening, you've probably heard the Peeper chorus chirping of metamorphosis and growing into their fullest potential. These wee frogs remind you to embrace your innate ability to evolve, especially when you think you've forgotten how. Peepers start life as tadpoles, then grow legs — and that's just part of their magic! Peeper also has a back-up plan for breathing: He can take in oxygen through his skin. Call on him when you've forgotten how to breathe and life feels impossible, or when you need to grow a new set of legs to carry you into your next becoming.

.... Ritual ....

STEP OUT OF YOUR ELEMENT

Spring Peepers (like all frogs) begin life as tadpoles. In his first few weeks, Frog will swim the shallows, propelled by a single flagellating tail, breathing through his gills like a fish.

As the weeks progress, he'll grow two rudimentary back legs, which will become powerful enough for him to jump great distances in a single bound. Then he grows front legs, each little froggy toe equipped with an adhesive pad so Frog can climb and cling. After about 12 weeks, Frog leaves the water to live on land. His transition complete, he can now breathe through his nose and absorb oxygen through his skin.

Spring Peeper can teach you to slip out of your comfort zone and swim away from your home pond to take in the view from the trees.

- Think about where you are comfortable, where you feel at home, where you can breathe easily.
- Now challenge yourself to do one thing that feels out of your element. If you're a homebody, try a dance class; if you're an extrovert, learn to knit. You don't have to make a lifelong commitment; simply create an opportunity to try something new. See how it alters the way you think, feel, and breathe!

THE RITES OF REINCARNATION

There are cultures that believe that we come back lifetime after lifetime, learning lessons that advance our soul. *But what if we reincarnate in this lifetime?* Think about this: In winter, Spring Peeper hunkers down in the mud at pond's edge and freezes into hibernation. In spring, he thaws to a new life.

What if we reinvent ourselves like the little Peeper frog, starting out as one thing and, through slow growth and effort, become something else?

By that definition, how many times have you reincarnated? How many "lifetimes" have you lived?

And how have you had to change, evolve, and grow as you moved from one state of being to the next?

That's what winter is: an exercise in remembering how to still yourself then how to come pliantly back to life again.

Ali Smith, *Winter*

Steady On

COMMON TORTOISE

Testudo graeca

Slow and steady, says Tortoise, well-versed in the ways of time. Tortoise was born ancient – older than Snake or Alligator and certainly older than humans. As other species have changed, evolved, and shifted, Tortoise has remained steadfast. Late to almost everything, Tortoise is the totem of the slow bloomer. *There's no need to be a prodigy*, Tortoise assures you. You didn't miss the boat simply because your first few decades have passed. Hunker down. Connect with the earth. Take a siesta. It's through the slow and steady that we truly come to know ourselves.

···· *Ritual* ····
SLOW YOUR ROLL

Tortoises are among the longest-lived creatures on earth, with life-spans sometimes measured in centuries. They have been associated with immortality not only because of their long lives but also because of Tortoise's ability to survive a forest fire — a gift given to those whose shells have thickened enough to withstand the heat. Tortoises are like stones, moving slowly so as not to disturb the flow of time.

What happens when you move more slowly?

Try this:

- Set the intention to take twice as long to eat a meal. Slow down your chewing and swallowing. Pause between bites. Put your fork down occasionally and breathe, noticing the world around you.

> *Tortoise or Turtle?*
> All tortoises are turtles, but not all turtles are tortoises. The word "tortoise" refers to land-dwelling creatures.

How does it feel to move more slowly, to step into tortoise time? Notice all the various parts of your being: How does your stomach feel? How does your mind feel? How does time itself feel?

····· *Reflection* ·····

A UNIVERSE UNTO HERSELF

Tortoise carries her home on her back. And that home, her shell, is often decorated with 13 scutes, the patterned squares of a tortoise shell. The 13 scutes are said to reflect the 13 full moons of the year. Thus, Tortoise represents both the earth, which she hugs with her powerful legs, and the night sky, which she wears on her back. She is a universe unto herself.

Tortoise is a solitary creature. Born alone, her mother long gone, she lives most of her life both inside her shell and deep in her burrow, which protects her from temperature changes. Tortoise teaches you the art of being at home with aloneness and with yourself.

How do you do with aloneness?

Can you come together with others, not from a place of need, but from the peace of your own center, contently balanced between your own earth and sky?

Loneliness is the poverty of self; solitude is richness of self.

May Sarton,
Journal of a Solitude

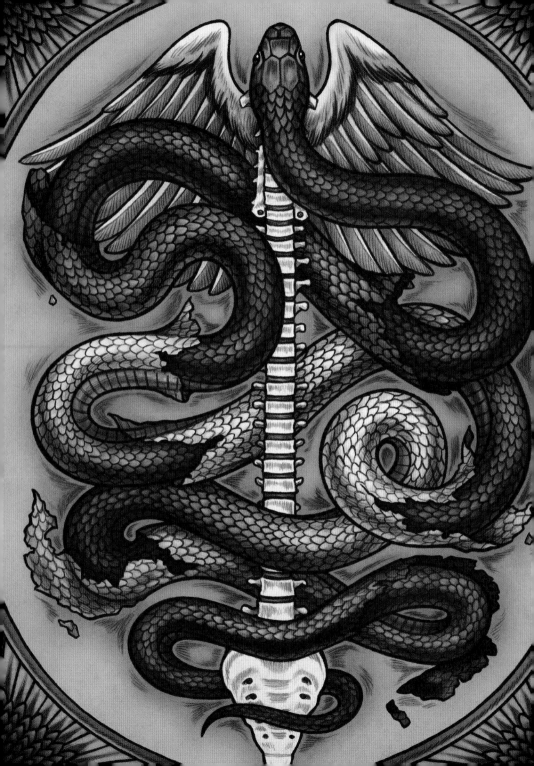

Grow Your Truth

BLACK SNAKE

Pantherophis obsoletus

Many moons ago, in a garden far away, Snake slid up to Eve and said, *You have a choice.* While Free Will isn't evil, it is complex. It requires each of us to define our own moral center and know what we stand for. Without this knowledge, it's easy to steer off course or be misled by smooth talkers and slick ideas. We grow when we see through the rhetoric and acknowledge our own truth. Each true choice expands you, until, as you outgrow who you used to be, your past begins to bind and itch. Black Snake slides in to remind you that growth requires release. She says, *Let go of what no longer serves so you can continue to expand into your truest self.*

···· *Ritual* ····
SHED YOUR SKIN

In order for Black Snake to grow, she must shed her skin. Unlike human skin, snake skin isn't stretchy enough to allow her to expand. So, a few times a year, Snake will shed. During these times, a film protects her eyes leaving her temporarily blind and vulnerable.

Growth and change often make us feel this way, too. Like Snake you may need to nest when you're shedding. You may feel metaphorically blind and unable to make smart decisions. Allow yourself space to feel into your new skin.

We humans initiate change with a mental shift. Ritualizing this shift allows us to move from the realm of pure thought and into the realm of the physical. When you begin to feel like you're outgrowing your current skin, bring a few cups of sea salt or a yummy bath scrub with you into the shower. As you scrub your skin, sloughing off old cells, think about what you need to release. Picture it being loosened by the salt so it can slide down the drain. Imagine what no longer serves you being washed away.

Black Snake will sometimes den with poisonous snakes like Copperheads. Call on her if you need to slide smoothly through a poisonous situation!

After Snake slides free of her constricting scales, she continues to expand until her outer casing chafes . . . and she begins the process again.

····· *Reflection* ·····

SNAKE MEDICINE

The Rod of Asclepius, Greek God of Healing, is a snake twining up a staff. In Hindu tradition, Kundalini energy — the raw power of creation — is symbolized by a snake moving up the spine and through the chakras. In the mountains of the Andes, the Anaconda represents the powerful life force of the physical world and the element of earth.

Yet Snake is one of our oldest monsters: She can move silently and her bite can kill. She is thought to be sly and deceitful, slippery and duplicitous, her forked tongue an indication that she may be two-faced.

How can Snake hold both healing and harm? This rich fullness is Snake's special magic. Her medicine is ancient, complex, and in many ways foundational because it represents a vast range of experiences and possibility.

What if Snake's forked tongue is not a sign of duplicity but instead indicates an ability to speak and know multiple truths simultaneously?

What if Snake's secret is that nothing is as cut-and-dried as we would like it to be, but that multiple realities exist at once until the moment you choose, and your choice creates the reality to come?

Can you see many sides of a situation, giving
each its due before making a decision?

Get Creative

SCREECH OWL

Megascops spp.

Clever Screech Owl has figured out how to get housekeeping service in her aerie: She brings a blind snake (a small creature who feeds on ants and flies) into her nest to eat the insects who would otherwise get into Owl's food stash. Screech Owl is endlessly creative. She'll play chameleon, blending into the trees, her feathers forming a near perfect imitation of bark. If she wants a little extra camouflage, she'll pretend to be a branch, making herself skinny and swaying gently so she looks like just another limb dancing in the breeze. When you hear Screech Owl trilling her melancholy song, it's time to get clever and creative with life's challenges.

..... *Ritual* .....

GET CREATIVE WITH YOUR PROBLEMS

Creativity says a snake can live in an owl's nest and an owl can imitate a tree.

In order to make these types of creative cognitive leaps, you need to shift out of your usual way of problem solving. If you're like most people, problem solving begins with thinking. Hard. Until your brains smells a bit like burnt rubber.

Let's give your brain a new way of working:

- Grab a pen and paper and draw your problems. This isn't about creating something beautiful. It's a way to shift the part of your brain that is doing the problem solving.
- Experiment to figure out what works best for you; you can create abstract drawings or comic strips. Try turning difficult concepts or emotions into pictures.

Expressing your feelings about a fight with your partner or decision about your job in images instead of words changes your thought patterns, which, in turn, gives you new and creative ways to approach problems.

Having a hard time putting pen to paper? Try collage!

····· *Reflection* ·····

RECOGNIZE YOUR CREATIVITY

Humans are infinitely creative and innovative . . . and that includes you. How does creativity play out in your life?

Are you a clever cook?

Do you create soulful social gatherings?

Can you fix just about anything with chopsticks, duct tape, and the spring from inside a ballpoint pen?

If you find yourself envious of other people's creativity, begin to notice how your own creativity expresses itself. Remember, it's not all about fine arts and poetry; creativity is ultimately about how we craft our daily lives.

You can't use up creativity. The more you use, the more you have.

Maya Angelou

Appreciate the Process
COW & BULL

Bos taurus

A lot of what Cow and Bull eat is indigestible to other animals. Cow and bull munch on field grass, undeterred by the tenacious fiber. After filling their bellies, they lie down to chew their cud, calmly working over the same meal, breaking it into smaller and smaller bits. Cows and Bulls, like good therapists, know how to process. They luxuriate in regurgitation and slow assimilation, taking what is unpalatable and making it into a full meal. To the ancients, this made them Gods and Goddesses, bringing fecundity in even the harshest conditions. For modern humans, Cow and Bull remind us to relax and appreciate process, the slow rumination that allows even the toughest problems to become digestible. Cow and Bull remind you that almost anything can be handled and assimilated if you give it time.

····· *Ritual* *·····*

APPRECIATE THE FOUNDATION

Nut, Egyptian Goddess of the Sky, was drawn as a cow with stars in her belly. Three different bull cults (dedicated to the Gods Apis, Mnevis, and Buchis) vied for followers during that same dynastic period. Cow and Bull were central to life in ancient Europe, India, and the Middle East. The bull symbolized aggressive fertility, the cow the feminine principal and fecundity; and oxen (castrated bulls) represented the methodical get-it-done attitude upon which these ancient civilizations were built.

Cow and Bull, among the first animals to be domesticated, have been living side-by-side with humans for more than 10,000 years. Civilizations were built on their backs. Yet, unless you live in India, Cow and Bull rarely get the respect given dogs or cats.

Like Cow and Bull, the people in our lives who are most foundational can easily be overlooked. Make this a week of gratitude: Notice, appreciate, and thank the people who support your daily existence. If you always say the words "thank you," take it further. Look the person in the eyes and add some energy to your words.

IS IT POSSIBLE THAT ALL IS WELL?

The German word *gemütlich* has been described as the feeling a cow has as it chews its cud in a field of wildflowers on a mild, sunny afternoon. Cow and Bull have mastered contentment of heart and spirit, at ease with themselves and with the world around them.

This is a true gift. Can you give it to yourself? Can you allow the world to be okay just as it is in this moment?

This is a big ask! Our brains are hardwired to notice problems, which is great for staying alive in a complex world but makes it difficult to cultivate happiness.

> *At some point, you gotta let go, and sit still, and allow contentment to come to you.*
>
> Elizabeth Gilbert,
> *Eat, Pray, Love*

What are the obstacles to your contentment?

Can you put these burdens down for a few moments of internal peace?

Sync with the Cycles
BLACK BEAR

Ursus americanus

On a half-moon night, watching Black Bear stretch up on her hind legs to climb your back fence, you might think for a moment that you have a very human burglar about to break in. Like us humans, Black Bear can stand tall, a conduit between earth and sky. Because of this, she is seen as our mirror-self, our wild sister tapped into healing wisdom and lush instinct. Black Bear connects deeply with the part of your psyche that longs to burrow under the blankets for the entirety of winter, and emerge blinking into the light with new projects clinging to your skirt like cubs. *Don't fight the cycles and seasons*, Black Bear teaches. Call on her to rediscover your rhythm and remember your wild.

···• *Ritual* •···
FOLLOW THE MOON

There is wisdom to be found in living in sync with the cycles of nature, even when (especially when!) you live in an urban environment. Black Bear reminds you to step into the cycles, letting their gentle flow shape your life.

To honor Black Bear, begin to get in sync with the cycles of the moon. Start simply: For one moon cycle, note the phase of the moon. Note where the moon is in the sky, where it rises, and where it sets.

During the next moon cycle, expand your practice. Add notes about your emotional and physical health as the moon moves through her phases. Are there certain times of the month when you're more easily joyous or more likely to be moved to tears?

As you continue this practice over time, you'll begin to know your own patterns, the cycles you flow through in sync with the moon's movements. This offers a certain predictability — an ability to foretell your own future — through knowing the seasons of your psyche.

An oracle is one who feels the patterns of time so deeply, she can peer into the future. Black Bear can connect you to the earth and sky's patterns, but it's you who connects to the practice that allows deepening into wisdom.

···• *Reflection* •···
STEP INTO THE DREAMING

As the nights get longer and the weather turns chill, Black Bear retreats into the dreaming. There's no guilt, no anxiety, no sense that she should be living any other way. Dark nights are for dreams and Black Bear knows this beyond all doubt.

We humans, on the other hand, fight the long night. We turn on lights, throw parties, and deny the time of dreams.

What happens if you give in to your natural rhythm, allowing longer sleep to punctuate your winter nights?

I like the night. Without the dark, we'd never see the stars.
Stephenie Meyer,
Twilight

What if this slowing, this deepening, this subtle sorrow, is the stuff of winter, to be embraced and accepted?

What happens if you invite Black Bear to come dream with you, bringing with her the deep healing of natural cycles?

Nurture Connections

GRAY WOLF

Canis lupis

Gray Wolf's power comes from understanding the intricacies of our bonds with each other. *Watch*, Wolf whispers, *let words and speech become background babble and, instead, focus on the eyes, the twitching muscles in the jaw* . . . Begin to feel into complex social situations, intuiting connections and relationships. This is how you learn who to trust – how you learn who leads.

Play and tend, Wolf reminds. This is how you build the bonds of tribe, a sense of wholeness. Wolf knows that you are a shimmering thread in a larger tapestry, part of an integral weaving of family and community. Understanding social dynamics and how to play them is Wolf's special medicine.

····· *Ritual* ·····
FIND YOUR VOICE

When Gray Wolf is lost and lonely, he howls to find his pack. When Wolf has a good hunt, he howls to share his joy. When Wolf howls, he doesn't worry whether he is singing on key; he doesn't care if his voice warbles. He simply expands and vibrates, opening his throat and, through it, his heart and mind.

Your throat connects your head with your heart. Opening your throat will help you feel connected and whole.

- Start by humming. You can hum a tune or just one note. Feel the air moving through your larynx, vibrating your being.

- Now try humming with your mouth open. Notice how this feels. Do your teeth vibrate?

- Next try toning: Create a single note, changing tone each time you take a new breath. Feel into each note. Notice if you feel it in your head or your throat or deep in your gut.

Are you scared to be heard?

Keep practicing opening your throat and perhaps one day you'll find yourself ready to howl!

···· *Reflection* ····
INDIVIDUAL OR PACK

In Cherokee culture, obsession with individuality is seen as sickness; wellness is derived from the pack, from the tribe. Because of this, when a member of the community becomes ill, healing must happen not only for the individual but also for family, friends, and the community.

Our culture demands individuality and achievement. Wolf teaches you to *be* pack. How can you reconcile these two concepts? How can you, like Wolf, create a life where you shine for both yourself and others?

Wolf is the wild brother of our longtime companion, Dog. Something in the human psyche longs for Wolf in the same way we might yearn for young, untamed love. We may fear it, but we also want the growth that discomfort can bring. Wolf is the wayfinder and teacher, but it's Dog who is the constant companion. Dog heals what we cannot heal within ourselves and protects us from things we can't sense or comprehend. People in the mountains of Peru often keep two dogs, one male and one female, to protect the masculine and feminine aspects (like the yin and yang) of the spirit. Dog teaches trust, and for millennia, Dog and Human have stayed true to one another.

Discover the Pattern

BROAD-WINGED KATYDID

Microcentrum rhombifolium

Like his cousin Cricket, Katydid has five eyes. He fixes them on life's intricacies, noticing details often missed by those of us with dual vision. From his perch atop the oak tree, he takes in the glow of the moon, the shadow of a tree limb, the stars burning holes in the night sky. These compounded images come together, coalescing into one, showing the slow evolution of the world as it changes. Details create patterns, patterns create rhythm. Katydid knows what's to come because he understands the design of what has been. When Katydid appears, look to the details so you, too, can begin to feel the rhythm and predict the future through the patterns of the present.

····· *Ritual* ·····

FINDING THE RHYTHM

All the members of Katydid's family, from Cricket to Grasshopper, are said to be able to predict storms. The syncopation of their song reflects changes in temperature, providing a rhythm appropriate for the season.

Katydid's song is actually percussive, coming not from his throat but from rubbing his forewings together. He hears his rhythm with "ears" located on his front legs. This nocturnal bard teaches us to find and celebrate the rhythms of the world around us.

The next time you hear the crickets and katydids playing their nightly tune, join them! Grab anything percussive: a drum, rattle, or tambourine; two sticks or wooden spoons; beans in a mason jar . . . it doesn't matter what you use.

Listen for the rhythm and join in. Match the beat. If you do this through the shifting seasons, you'll begin to notice changes in the nightly rhythm. Do these changes correlate with weather changes? With shifts in the moon's phase?

Notice if you feel any differently or if you notice things in a new way, now that you've joined the cosmic chorus.

SEEING THROUGH MANY EYES

Having compound eyes is like sitting in a control room watching video feeds that show the same situation from many angles. Each micro-eye records an image, and then Katydid's brain combines the images into a cohesive story. Added to this are impressions of light and dark, which are the specialty of three additional eyes called ocelli.

We miss so much with our one set of eyes, actually and metaphorically. We put a lot of faith in what we can see, but can you think of times when your eyes have not showed you the entirety of a situation? Or when you missed an important detail?

What would happen if you shifted the way
you looked at the world, looking for long-term
patterns instead of short-term moments?

Can you put your personal beliefs and prejudices
aside and see the world through another's eyes?

While there is perhaps a province in which the
photograph can tell us nothing more than what we
see with our own eyes, there is another in which it
proves to us how little our eyes permit us to see.

Dorothea Lange

Love Fiercely

WHOOPER SWAN

Cygnus cygnus

In the darkness of year's end, Swan flies north. North is where the spirits gather, so Swan willingly carries with her the souls of the recently departed. She loves them as fiercely and tenderly as she loves her own mate — and so sees them all the way home. Some say that when she returns in spring, a wisp of those she carried clings to her, a mirror and a memory, making Swan feel like family, like kin, to those who have loved and lost. Perhaps that's why we sometimes see Swan rising from the lake, shape-shifting into the form of our beloved, demanding the sacrifices that only the fiercest love can fathom. Swan reminds us that when we love fiercely, our love is never truly lost.

···· *Ritual* ····

CHOOSE LOVE AGAIN

Swan is woven into our world myths, teaching us of love that is, above all, tenacious.

Swan tends to stick it out, mating for life, and learning year after year how to live in partnership. This doesn't mean it's easy. Swan migrates vast distances (some biologists say this pattern allows for little time to change mates!) and she and her partner will start a new family every year and raise the cygnets together.

How do you find the strength and endurance for this kind of love? Sometimes it's as simple as choosing it over and over again.

Either before bed at night or first thing in the morning, choose your love anew. Whether this is the love of a person, a pet, a project, or yourself, put your hands on your heart, take a few deep breaths, and remember why you love what you love.

In ancient Celtic cultures, marriages were set for a limited duration, giving the couple the opportunity to choose whether to stay or go at the end of the contracted time. Give yourself this same freedom of choice every day.

WILL LOVE CHANGE YOU?

Many moons ago a young hero named Angus fell in love. He fell hard and fast and forever, which was odd because he had only ever seen his true love when she visited his dreams.

Caer haunted his nights, singing to his heart 'til he was sick with love. But, seeing her only in dreamtime, he had no idea she was the daughter of the Faerie King.

Angus was listless and useless, wanting only to sleep and dream so he could be with Caer. Fed up, Angus's father sent him on a quest to find this mystery woman. Angus searched and sought and finally found her, quickly realizing she was no mortal woman but a Faerie Princess.

Angus approached the Faerie King and asked if he could court her. The King snickered, "Good luck with that, lad! She's a wild one. Oh, and by the way, she spends half the year as a swan." The Faerie King didn't realize the power of love to change both wild women and young heroes.

Are you willing to transform yourself
to understand the one you love?

Angus was. He spent half the year as a swan, flying with Caer and her swan maidens . . . And they lived happily ever after.

How will love change you?

Work Together

HOUSE MOUSE

Mus musculus

Mouse is unobtrusive, slipping between cracks and scurrying behind walls. We notice her by the destruction she leaves behind: chewed wires and ruined books, food made inedible to us by her munching. Mouse churns through paper at an enviable rate, destroying in hours what it took years to create. That's because Mouse rarely goes it alone – she has help. Mouse breeds prolifically: where there is one there are sure to be more. And once you have not *mouse* but *mice*, it's mind-boggling what havoc these small creatures can wreak. *Work together*, Mouse advises; *you don't have to be big to be mighty.*

Find Your Element

SEA TURTLE

Chelonia mydas

On the beaches of her birth, Sea Turtle is frustratingly awkward. She paddles for purchase in the slippery sand, which she returns to only to lay her eggs. Even this is not a yearly practice; her homecoming happens only every few years when she can no longer resist the call of her home beach. The rest of the time she is a creature of water, smoothly swimming great distances and frolicking in the sun-drenched ocean. While birth delivered her to the sandy shore, this ancient creature is most herself when out of her element. Water is her true home, the place where she is quick and graceful and joyous. If you feel uncomfortable in your natal family or place of origin, call on Sea Turtle to help you find your natural element.

····· *Ritual* ·····
TONING YOUR TOLERANCE

Turtles are ectotherms, meaning they get heat from without instead of producing it within. Unlike us humans who need to keep it close to 98 degrees, Sea Turtle can handle a wide range of external and internal temperatures. Conditioning yourself to a wider range of temperature tolerance can benefit your health and build your ability to adapt to life's ongoing changes.

Create two footbaths, one comfortably hot and one cold. Put your feet in the hot one for about 30 seconds; then move them to the cold for 10 seconds. Move back and forth between the temperatures at least five times.

Want more of a full-body experience? At the end of a shower, make the water as cold as you can bear for 10 seconds before going back to your normal temperature. Do this a few times before you get out of the shower.

Learning to quiet the protests of your mind through the discomfort of these temperature changes is a skill you can use when you have to adapt to other uncomfortable changes in your life. Toning your tolerance will help you, like Sea Turtle, to travel and see the world, adjusting to whatever circumstances you find yourself in.

THE DREAM OF FREEDOM

Unlike her terrestrial cousins, Sea Turtle is almost always on the move. She can swim thousands of miles before returning to her natal shore to lay her eggs. Because Sea Turtle can store the sperm of her mate for up to three years, she inseminates each clutch of eggs with sperm mixed from various lovers. After she lays her eggs, she moves on, leaving the baby turtles to be raised by instinct and nature.

There is a part of each of us that longs for this type of freedom: freedom of place, and from family or responsibility. We long to remake our lives out of different stuff than their current fabric in the same way Sea Turtle sloughs off the sandy shore for the joy of the sea.

Our human way is to feel guilty and repress these emotions when they arise.

But what if you allow these emotions to surface?

What if you allow yourself the freedom to dream everything and anything . . . and then pick up your responsibilities anew, choosing and appreciating each aspect of your life?

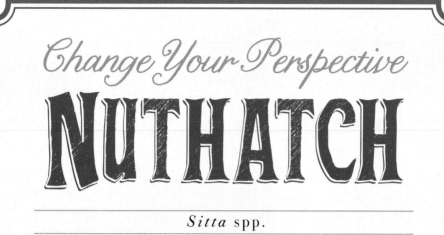

Change Your Perspective

NUTHATCH

Sitta spp.

Up is down and down is up. To Nuthatch, it really doesn't matter. This little bird has no trouble when life gets topsy-turvy. A backward pointing toe lets this quirky friend walk down tree trunks while other birds can only climb up. Is Nuthatch simply being contrarian, or is going against the grain serving some special purpose? Here's a hint: When you flip everything over, the world looks dramatically different. This allows Nuthatch to store his winter seed stash in plain sight for him; but to other birds, it's hidden by folds in the bark. Nuthatch reminds you to approach your usual problems from a different direction. A change of perspective makes all the difference!

···· *Ritual* ····

FIND A NEW APPROACH

Other birds, while hopping up a great tree's trunk, never notice Nuthatch's stash of seeds cleverly deposited in bark pockets that can be seen only when heading down.

We often approach problems in our lives from one direction. But what happens if you flip the problem over or find a back door? Let's use the cards that come with this book to find out!

Hold the cards in your hands and think of a problem, conflict, or issue you're currently working through. Set the intention to draw a card that will help you approach this issue from a different angle, so you can see both the issue and the solution in a new way.

Shuffle or fan the cards with the backs facing you (no cheating!) and draw whichever one feels right. Then ask yourself how the energy of the animal you are looking at can help with your particular issue. Does this animal give you a new way to approach your problem?

···· *Reflection* ····

AGAINST THE FLOW

There are patterns in all of our lives. Some of them are simple — like which side of the road to drive on — and others are more obscure, more felt than thought. Some of these patterns are social contracts that keep us safe; others are habits with roots that have been lost in the twists and turns of time and culture.

We tend to be reactive when someone goes against the grain. Think of the person who pushes backward against the crowd, goes up the down escalator, or moves against the flow of pedestrian traffic in an airport. What thoughts cross your mind as you get out of the way?

How do you treat people who go against the grain?

Do you let yourself move against the flow?

*What's the difference between a rebel
and an innovator?*

····································

*Innovation distinguishes between
a leader and a follower.*

Steve Jobs

Stand Up for Yourself

SPOTTED SKUNK

Spilogale spp.

While Spotted Skunk may be known for causing a stink, smelling up the room is really a last resort. First, she goes big, standing on her front legs, fanning her tail in the air, and stomping forward so she seems fierce and imposing. Skunk can make herself appear larger than her naturally diminutive stature, glamouring even the toughest customers into leaving her alone. Here's the thing: While Spotted Skunk doesn't back down, the harm she creates is pure illusion. Sure, the unwary will be stinky for a stretch but Skunk stands up for herself without causing permanent damage. Can you find a way to both stand up for yourself and do no harm?

····· *Ritual* ·····
TRAIN YOUR NOSE

We are constantly taking in scents in our daily lives, but it's only the strongest or most unusual smells that grab our attention. Spotted Skunk knows that scent is a powerful tool for self-defense. To harness the power of scent, you have to train your nose first to notice scent and then to recognize it. Try this:

Choose 3 to 5 essential oils to work with. You don't have to like the smell of them! Start by taking off the bottle caps and shuffling them around so you don't know which is which. Then, use your nose to pick which cap goes with which bottle. Look at the name of the oil only after you've matched cap to bottle. Do this a few days in a row so you begin to know the oils by scent as much as by name.

Try to identify similarities between the scents. If two scents seem similar, research them to see if you can identify the component you're smelling. Both eucalyptus and lavender contain camphor, for example. Once you notice the similarity in scent, you'll be able to identify it in other places as well.

Like learning a new language, scent may feel completely foreign in the beginning. Allow yourself to play and experiment as you develop this sense.

···· *Reflection* ····
HOW DO YOU HANDLE CONFLICT?

Each of us has a style we revert to when we feel cornered. Some of us, like Possum, play dead; others will attack like Grizzly; and there are those who will turn tail like Rabbit.

When it comes to handling conflict, Spotted Skunk is a profound teacher. Despite her diminutive stature, she doesn't back down, fluffing herself up to appear much larger than she is. Think of it as "pulling an aura," this ability to feel energetically and spiritually bigger than your physical body.

Tiny Spotted Skunk doesn't run from a fight. In fact, it's usually the big, bad predator who says, *Sorry, Ma'am, I confused you with someone else. I'll just be on my way.*

Even when she causes a stink, Spotted Skunk doesn't cause permanent harm. Instead, she assaults the senses, convincing even Bear and Wolf that they'd be happier if they left her alone.

How do you handle conflict? Do your methods achieve your goals?

What can you learn from Spotted Skunk?

Listen for Spirit

BARN OWL

Tyto alba

On a dark-moon night, Barn Owl swoops low over the fields. Her wingbeats are not only nearly silent but create a wake of quietude, a vortex of otherness. Crossing her path feels like crossing over into elsewhere. And so, Barn Owl has long been a messenger between the worlds, bringing word from the realm of spirits and ghosts. Barn Owl hunts even on the darkest nights, her ears picking up the small chattering of mice and the soft sound of grass brushing against a rabbit's skin . . . or maybe she simply senses their souls as they go about their nightly business. _Close your eyes,_ Barn Owl whispers, _and open your ears to the sound of spirit._

····· *Ritual* ·····
JOURNEY TO SPIRIT

Barn Owl reminds you to connect with and find guidance in the whisperings of spirit that live within your own heart. This simple meditation journey will help you reconnect with your own spirit spark.

- Begin by getting comfortable either sitting or lying down. Breathe in and out through your nose, allowing your body to relax.
- Now imagine your consciousness slipping outside of your body, stepping out of your own skin.
- Glide around so you are standing behind yourself. Imagine a small door behind your heart. Open that door and step inside.
- What does it look like on the pathway to your heart? What does it smell and sound like?
- Walk in farther until you come to the chamber where your spirit lives. Notice your surroundings. Notice how your spirit looks.
- Ask Spirit if it has a message for you, then listen with your whole being. Call on Barn Owl to help you hear truly.
- When you are finished, walk out to the door, close it, and seal it behind you.
- Walk back around to your front and step back into your own skin.

Journal what you noticed right away, before you lose the sense of your journey.

LEARNING TO LISTEN

Sometimes, in order to strengthen one sense, we need to dampen another. We're very used to approaching the world through our eyes. We often need to "see it with our own eyes" in order to believe. Barn Owl reminds us that sight isn't the only way to connect. Intuition and inner-knowing can't be seen with your eyes.

How do you define what's real for you?

Does your intuition have a seat at the decision-making table?

How do you work with the information you receive in dreams and meditations?

Insight is not a lightbulb that goes off inside our heads. It is a flickering candle that can easily be snuffed out.

Malcolm Gladwell,
Blink: The Power of Thinking Without Thinking

Dive Under the Surface

ORCA

Orcinus orca

When you look at the ocean or the surface of a lake, the first thing you see is a reflection of the sky. The water's surface is a mirror, hiding the depths. When you dive deep, you discover there are worlds within worlds below that mirrored surface. Underwater is its own magical kingdom, a world with love and song and family. In the language of the Lummi Nation of the Pacific Northwest, the word for Orca translates as "the people beneath the sea." Orca holds up a mirror, showing us another possible world, one with different ways of communicating and creating family. Orca asks, *What is possible when you dive under the surface? Are there other ways to live and be? Can you create an alternate world for yourself?*

···· *Ritual* ····
FEEL THE VIBRATION

Orca communicates and navigates through sound. Whistles, which don't carry long distances underwater, are used for private communication while pulsed calls are used to communicate to the entire pod. Orca in the same pod share a common dialect, or group of sounds, to communicate with one another.

Orca finds her way around through echolocation — the echo from a series of sounds helps her determine distances and the location of objects to navigate. We humans know the way sound carries through the air. It's completely different under water. Next time you take a bath or are at a pond or swimming pool, put your head underwater and experiment with making different noises.
Feel the vibration in your head and jaw.
Notice how sound bounces
(or doesn't) in the water.

If you want to find the secrets of the universe, think in terms of energy, frequency, and vibration.

Nikola Tesla

····· *Reflection* ·····
GREATER KINSHIP

Orca are the largest animals of the dolphin clan. Like their well-loved bottlenose cousins, they are social and gregarious, living in large family units called pods that travel, hunt, and play together. Orca are also the ocean's version of the canary in the coal mine. As the canary's health gives a clue to the air quality in a mine shaft, Orca's health hints at the health of the waters in which she lives.

During the summer of 2018, a female Orca called Tahlequah carried the body of her dead calf for more than 17 days, pushing it to the surface while she circled on a "tour of grief."

Tahlequah is part of what's known as the Southern Resident pod, and they are living in polluted water. Chinook salmon, the pod's main food source, are dying due to the damming of rivers. The increasing sounds of boats are making it difficult for Orca to navigate. Some say Tahlequah was not only mourning but also showing her human kin what is happening to the oceans, breaking the surface of the water to show us what is going on in the depths.

Can you feel kinship for those outside your pod?

What would you be willing to change in your life to restore harmony between different worlds?

Make Manifest
BEAVER

Castor canadensis

Beaver doesn't just sit around thinking. He plans, then executes, carefully damming up waterways to construct the ponds and swamplands where he builds his island home. And that home? It's a marvel of modern engineering with an underwater entrance, snug dry bedrooms, and plenty of storage for winter foodstuffs. Beaver knows how to fundamentally change landscapes, bringing water to barren areas. Call on Beaver when you are ready for foundational change, whether remaking an inner-landscape or creating something new in the world at large. Beaver teaches us not only how to make manifest, moving from thought to reality, but how to plan for the future. Whatever you hope to accomplish, call on Beaver's medicine to help you go from idea to done.

···· *Ritual* ····

CLEAR SPACE FOR AN ALTAR

Creating an altar is an act of designating sacred space. It's a place for honoring, meditation, reflection, and for dreaming. Here's how to build yours:

FIND A PLACE TO BUILD YOUR ALTAR. You can put an altar on top of the fridge or in a box under the bed — don't get too precious about this! Use the fireplace mantle, a windowsill, a corner of your desk, or an old stump in the yard. You declaring, "this is sacred space," makes it a sacred space.

CLEAN YOUR SPOT! Maybe that means soap and water, or maybe you want to cleanse it energetically by burning sage, cedar, mugwort, or your favorite incense. The idea is to create a blank canvas to which you can purposefully add things. The clearing off is also part of the consecration: the energetic act of turning something mundane, like a tabletop, into something sacred.

Elemental symbols — such as a candle for fire, a bowl of water for water, a plant for earth, or a feather for air — can be placed on your altar to represent the material stuff out of which everything is made. The elements also represent you. Earth is your body, air your breath, water emotion, and fire is spirit. Representing the elements on your altar brings you to this sacred space.

····• *Reflection* •····
WHAT'S SACRED TO YOU?

The next step in creating your altar is to reflect on what's sacred to you right now, knowing this will change over time. Perhaps today you're thinking about your lineage, and your ancestors feel near and sacred. Next week you might be working with animal medicine and using your altar as a place to reflect on that energy.

Think of your altar as a workspace for your spiritual doings.

What you put on your altar will depend on what you are currently working on spiritually. Remember, this space needs to be sacred to no one but you. Add things to your altar beginning on the eastern side and moving westward to honor the movement of the sun. You could also place items in a clockwise pattern to build energy, or a counter-clockwise pattern if the altar is meant to unwind an energy or situation. You might want to include a candle, statue, crystal, or bowl of water as a focal point for quiet reflection. Making an altar is a creative act, so feel into it! Finally, notice how you built your altar. Is it symmetrical or asymmetrical? Is it sparse or full? Simply use this to gather information about yourself and your current energy (no judgment!).

Everything Is Connected

ZIGZAG SPIDER

Argiope aurantia

Spider crouches on her web, feeling the strands of creation. *Everything is connected*, she murmurs. *And understanding those connections is key.* So, while Spider seems to be sitting on her web waiting for dinner, she's actually taking the temperature of the world and listening for connection. When the breeze ruffles the web's threads, Spider senses the force and direction. The morning dew is thick, Spider sees; she knows that autumn is upon us and beyond that winter, when flies are scarce. Your world, too, is a web. Pause a moment and feel the play on the different strands and how that affects the overall weaving. Spider reminds you to be still and take the time to understand interconnections.

····• *Ritual* •····

ENERGIZE YOUR INTENTIONS

An intention is part of a web of energy, action, and relationships. Spider, the ultimate web builder, can help you explore the art of intending. But be careful! Fairy tales teach us that getting exactly what we ask for can end up not being what we really want. Before you energize your intention, it is wise to first hop over to the Reflection here to help you get clear on your goals and the ripple effects. Once you've explored your intention, you can begin to energize it.

Imagine you are Spider, sitting in your web:

- Set up an altar with your intention as its focus (don't know how to build an altar? Turn to Beaver on page 95). Know that every time you work on your intention altar, you are energizing your desires. You can do this by making an offering: a lit candle, a song, or a prayer. You could meditate or offer Reiki, giving a little bit of energy to the intention held in your web.

- Use symbols to energize your intention. If you are intending to attract love, you might burn rose petals.

- Create a ritual to symbolize bringing your intention into being. Many of our cultural rituals fall into this category: a wedding sets an intention for the future of the couple, a birthday party carries wishes for the year to come.

····• *Reflection* •····
CONSIDER YOUR WEB

Spider knows everything is interconnected, that pulling one strand of the web can affect the shape of the whole. An intention, and the actions that make it happen, creates a strong pull on the web of which you are a part. So, before you begin doing the work of manifesting an intention, carefully examine the cause and effect your intention will put in motion. Nothing happens in a vacuum! Consider your web of effect with a process called mindmapping:

On a blank piece of paper:

- Identify your intention and place it in a circle at the center of the page. This is the core of your web.
- Each in its own circle, begin writing all the things which will be affected by putting your intention in motion. For example, if you intend to do yoga 3 times a week, there is a ripple effect that might reach your partner, kids, job, and even the yoga teacher.
- Consider your intention's relationship to family, friends, finances, career, home, spiritual life, and other areas of your world. Be thorough in your investigation! There is yin and yang to everything . . . examine both the bright side and the shadow.

Now that you've identified how your intention might affect the world around you, you can begin the manifestation process.

Free Your Inner Fire

PILEATED WOODPECKER

Dryocopus pileatus

Woodpecker drums with abandon. He'll tap on trees, rain gutters, and garbage cans, his noise a gift from the Thunder Gods themselves. Can you give yourself over to this type of passion? Can you dance the primal rhythm that calls the rain? Our critical minds often get in the way of our creativity and joy. A big part of your brain's job is to keep you safe, and giving in to passion can be dangerous. But Woodpecker has a secret: He wraps his tongue around his brain to protect it from his concussive rhythm. Woodpecker is calling you to get in sync, to move and dance and drum. How can you free your inner fire?

···· *Ritual* ····
FIND YOUR BEAT

Woodpecker's rhythm is said to be the heartbeat of Mother Earth.

- Find your own heartbeat. Put your right hand over your heart and feel for its thrum. Sit with it, allowing the feeling to swell into your veins.

- Having trouble feeling your heartbeat? Find it in the pulse in your neck or wrist.

- See if you can imitate the rhythm vocally. Snap it. Tap it out with a pen.

Woodpecker uses his beat to find food, find love, communicate, and defend his territory. We all have a unique beat, a rhythm that is ours and ours alone. Find your beat, let your hips sway with it, let it be foundational to who you are and who you want to become.

Only man is permitted to live without rhythm in order that he can become free. However, he must of his own accord bring rhythm again into the chaos.

Rudolf Steiner

GOING BIG

Pileated Woodpecker is energetically huge. He's noisy, he's got a bright red tuft on the top of his head, and he's a dang big bird. Because Woodpecker gets agitated before storms, he has been associated with the clap of thunder. When Woodpecker appears, expect big movement in your life. Notice what feels out of sync or not in flow to help you know the direction from which the storm is coming.

If Woodpecker brings big thunder, he also brings the medicine to help you through it. That medicine is rhythm. Rhythm can mean many things. It can literally be music, dance, or the beat of the drum, but it can also be daily and seasonal routines. Rhythm can mean living in sync with the cycles of the moon or having a daily gratitude practice.

What rhythms do you have in place to help you through life's thunderstorms?

What routines can you fall back on when life feels topsy-turvy?

What practices no longer serve you, but you keep doing them because you're in the rhythm?

Honor Lineage

ASIAN ELEPHANT

Elephas maximus

Elephant stands in the river of time, honoring the past and nurturing the future, always feeling the lines of lineage radiating both forward and back. She remembers her ancestors, the mastodons and the mammoths, the long-extinct cousins in this ancient family, and knows she is a link in the chain of life. Her daughters will someday be matriarchs and then mere bone, fossils that will someday point to a species that no longer exists. You, too, are a link, a bridge between what came before and what is yet to come. As you move through your life, honor not only what is past but what is yet to be.

· · ·● Ritual ●· · ·

HONOR YOUR LINEAGE

Where do you come from and where is your lineage headed? This is a complex and layered question. There is family and intellectual lineage, plus geographic wanderings. There are religious practices, recipes, songs, and poems in a long trail that stretches not only behind you but into the future.

Begin exploring:

- Old photographs
- Your DNA
- Maps, tracing the routes of movement and migration
- Family recipes
- Stories and songs
- People who have shaped your personal philosophy and morality (intellectual and emotional lineage is often not tied to blood)

Dream into the future, seeking your children's children — this can be as simple as setting the intention before you go to bed, and look at your choices: How will they affect the future of your lineage?

Choose a way to honor your lineage. This might be creating an altar (see Beaver on page 95) or making a family feast or taking a pilgrimage to a place your ancestors lived. Remember you are a living link in a long and ever-changing chain.

···· *Reflection* ····
LOSING CONTROL

Elephant has only a few teeth at a time. When her front teeth wear out, the back ones move forward to replace them and new back teeth grow in their place.

Symbolically, strong teeth are associated with feeling in control of your life. If you've ever had a panicky dream in which your teeth were knocked out, some part of your waking life was probably feeling out of control. But Elephant expects to lose her teeth. There is no panic, only calm acceptance of change.

Is it your nature to try to control the details of your life? How does this make you feel?

Can you flow with life's uncertainties like Elephant?

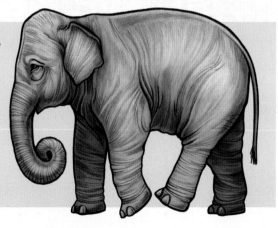

Elephant displays incredible grace despite her size, and amazing insight despite having poor eyesight. Call on Elephant when you need to be comfortable in your own skin despite what others may see as a deficiency.

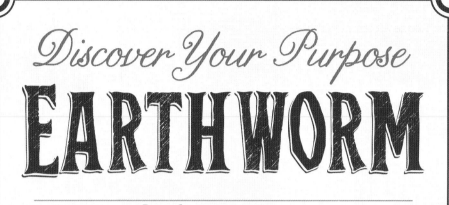

Discover Your Purpose
EARTHWORM

Lumbricus terrestris

Life is straightforward when you know your purpose. While Earthworm may seem a simple creature, she knows her purpose well: She brings life. Earthworm wriggles through the soil, creating space for air and water, which is the lifeblood of dirt. Minerals wriggle through Earthworm's body, getting digested so they are more available when the trees and plants come looking for a meal. Earthworm even regenerates herself, growing new sections when bits have been lopped off by a careless shovel. Regeneration is Earthworm's life purpose and daily work. What's your daily work? Earthworm reminds you that life is simpler when you connect your daily doings with your greater purpose.

····• *Ritual* •····

CONNECTING WITH PURPOSE

Sometimes it's hard to believe that there is a greater purpose beyond paying the bills and putting food on the table. But what happens when, for a few minutes a day, you believe your soul has a purpose in this lifetime?

- Find a comfortable and quiet place to sit or lie down.
- Breathe slow and steady, following your breath in and out, imagining your inner-self as a still, clear lake. You can see your reflection in the water, rippling as the lake breathes with you.
- Now, imagine a pebble tossed into the lake. It's a small pebble and it bears this question: *What's my purpose?*
- See what images arise as the pebble changes the ripples on the water creating pictures.
- As you come slowly back to yourself, record what you saw.

Over a series of days or weeks, put together an image to answer your question. Discard directives as messages from ego and focus on metaphor and imagery.

Be Ready for Unexpected Answers

When you ask soul questions, you get soul answers, which are not always comfortable. Be aware that the answer you get may not suit your ego or your current lifestyle!

• • • •  • • • •

ARE YOU BALANCED?

Earthworm's presence is a sign of healthy soil. Why? Because she brings balance to the four elements — earth, air, water, and fire. Here's how:

By wriggling through the soil, Earthworm creates tubes through which air and water enter the Earth, keeping it from becoming dense and compacted.

By digesting large minerals, Earthworm helps the earth compost and assimilate. Digestion is an attribute of fire.

So, Earthworm brings balance by adding the elements the Earth might be missing.

You, too, need to stay in elemental balance.

- Earth is your body, your material being.

- Air is breath and thought.

- Fire is digestion, passion, and creativity.

- Water is emotion and reflection.

*Do you have missing elements
that you need to call into balance?*

What would bring your whole being into balance?

Renew Your Life

SEA EAGLE

Haliaeetus albicilla

When Old Eagle can no longer spot pike jumping in the sea, when her wings feel heavy and slow, she remembers the lore of reincarnation. This mystery is passed down to those of her kind who, as fledglings, are strong enough to look straight into the fiery sun. As the ancient knowing rises in her soul, Eagle finds a well of clear, clean water. With that well as her tether to Earth, she leaps skyward and sunward, flying up 'til her feathers sear and the fog is burned from her eyes. Then she plummets back to earth, into the depths of the well's water, emerging renewed. Eagle reminds us that life moves in cycles. When you get tired and burned out, draw on the wisdom of your soul to find renewal.

····•• *Ritual* ••····

BRING FIRE TO YOUR HEART

Eagle flies close to the sun, the birthplace of fire. Fire, representing creativity and kinetic energy, brings passion and warmth. Call on Fire, and bring it into your heart to spark renewal and regeneration.

This is a beautiful ritual to perform in front of a fire, but a candle will do in a pinch.

- Begin by closing your eyes. Let the light dance on your lids, warming your sight.

- Breathe in the warm air, feeling it in your mouth and lungs.

- Hold up your hands, letting the heat seep into your palms.

- Then (carefully!) imagine gathering the light in your hands and pulling it toward you.

- First, gather the light and pull it toward your eyes that your vision may be clear.

- Next, gather the light and pull it toward your navel, the center of creativity.

- Finally, pull the light to your chest, letting it warm your heart – softening, sparking, and clarifying.

- Sit with the fire until you feel complete.

···· *Reflection* ····
WHAT'S CLOUDING YOUR VISION?

Eagle's medicine is not for the faint of heart. Eagle flies higher than any bird, closer to the sun and closer to spirit. When you call on Eagle, you call on the fire of your own soul. And when you call on Sea Eagle, you are balanced between the watery depths and the fiery sky.

This is not a gentle renewal: you become strong like fire-forged steel tempered in cool water.

What in your life needs to be burned off?

What's clouding your vision?

What's keeping you from seeing clearly and flying true?

We must be willing to get rid of the life we've planned, so as to have the life that is waiting for us. The old skin has to be shed before the new one can come.

Joseph Campbell

Transcend Yourself
ANDALUSIAN
HORSE

Equus ferus

While it's well known that Horse can carry your body, what's less known is that Horse can transport your soul. In times past, if you wanted to visit your sister in the next village you called on Horse; and when you wanted to visit your great-grandmother in the lands beyond, you also called on Horse. Horse is a companion and guide whose gift is the freedom to transcend physical incarnation. Whether your body needs to move through space or your soul needs to glide through time, Horse beckons you to your journey. When you're not sure you can make it there alone, call on Horse to carry you. Horse says, *it's time to transcend your current way of being.*

···· *Ritual* ····

JOURNEY BEYOND

Asiatic shamans call their drum a "horse" because the vibrations help them travel to realities beyond the physical one. You, too, can travel beyond your physical self. Start by searching the internet for "shamanic journey drumming track." Drumming helps the brain slip into a theta wave pattern, which lets your mind journey beyond the confines of everyday consciousness.

Lie down or sit comfortably. Set a guiding intention for your journey, such as, "I want to connect with my spirit animal."

Play the drumming track and think about a place in nature that is comfortable and familiar. In your mind, create a door from that place into the Earth. Open the door and step through, imagining yourself traveling downward into the heart of the world.

Use all your senses to become aware of this dream space. Time may pass quickly, and you'll be surprised when you hear the "call back" sequence, which is when the drumming rhythm speeds up to let you know it's time to return.

Retrace your steps, coming back the same way you went in. Be sure to close the door behind you to separate your waking life from the subconscious realms of the journey. Spend a few minutes noting your experience while fresh in your mind, capturing details like color, symbol, and archetypes.

····· *Reflection* ·····
MELDING INTO ONE

Our alliance with Horse drastically changed the course of human history. Distances became crossable and loads were haulable. And so, Horse became associated with journeys both in this world and in the dreamworlds. Horse is a companion and guide and, perhaps more importantly, horse is a catalyst, making the journey possible. Thus, Horse represents freedom.

Horse lends us strength and stamina, and gives form to our passion and purpose. The experience of riding on Horse's back also allows us to experience oneness with something outside of ourselves. Transcending our individual humanity and melding with Horse is represented by the mythical centaur, which had a horse's body and a human torso and head.

Many of us long for this kind of melding, this sense of transcendence, but also fear giving up our individuality.

Can you come together with another and still be yourself?

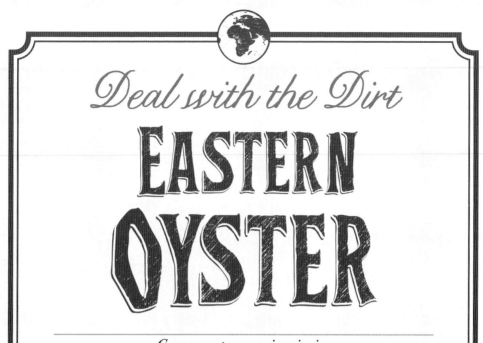

Deal with the Dirt

EASTERN OYSTER

Crassostrea virginica

Life is messy, but that doesn't bother Oyster. Water pollution? No problem. Oyster will filter it, package it up, and send it to the bottom of the sea. Grit and sand? Easy-peasy. Oyster will cover it with layer upon layer of nacre until it shines. Oyster's magic is knowing how to deal with the dirt. If this unlikely animal ally is appearing, see what's gotten grungy. Is your home a mess? Your partnerships? Your thoughts? Look within and decide what you need to filter out and what you'll keep and transform into your own pearl.

···· *Ritual* ····

BODY CLEANSE

Call in Oyster energy by supporting your body's multi-tiered filtration system with this light-weight, full body cleanse. Try this for one week:

- In the morning, drink 8 ounces of water mixed with one teaspoon of flax, chia, or psyllium seed to support the bowel and aid in clearing toxins from the colon.

- Over the course of the day drink at least 64 ounces of water with a squeeze of lemon or lime. Water helps the kidneys and bladder excrete urine, which removes waste from the blood. Citric acid from the lemon or lime can give your digestive system a boost.

- Before you shower, dry brush your skin to help stimulate the lymphatic system. During your shower, use hot water to bring on a sweat, then switch to cold water, alternating back and forth twice. This hot-cold action is thought to tone the blood vessels so they can continue the work of carrying nutrients and moving toxins out.

- For 5 minutes in the evening, practice deep and conscious breath-ing to support healthy lung function.

If you occasionally do a big detox, see how it feels to make like Oyster and do a light detox on a more regular basis.

···· *Reflection* ····
TOXIC THOUGHTS

There's an old Taoist fable that goes like this:

A man comes to a Taoist monk and says, "I'm new to this village. Will I be happy here?" The monk asks, "Were you happy in your old village?" The man says, "Oh yes!" And the monk replies, "Then you will be happy here."

Another man comes to the monk and asks the same question: "I just moved here. Will I be happy in this village?" Again, the monk asks, "Were you happy in your old village?" The man replies, "No." The monk pauses before saying, "Then I don't know that you'll be happy here."

Our thoughts shape our experience of life. If you are constantly entertaining toxic thoughts, it is hard to be happy. Notice if you are comparing yourself to others, always feeling like you're not enough or you don't have enough, blaming other people for your troubles, or spending your energy trying to change the people you love.

> *The pearl is the oyster's autobiography.*
>
> Federico Fellini

Noticing these types of thought patterns? Turn your toxic thoughts into pearls with a gratitude practice. (See River Otter on page 155.)

Navigate by the Sun

HONEYBEE

Apis mellifera

Honeybee flies a zigzag path, searching for patches of pollen. When she finds one, she flies home to the hive where she dances to let the others know the pollen's location. Honeybee is efficient in this aerial charade, showing with her body the exact angle that the sun hits the pollen patch. Her sisters triangulate the location so that they can join in the feast. Bee's internal compass is incredibly accurate. She can find the sun, even on a cloudy day. The sun has traditionally represented expansive, moving energies — our passions and our ability to make those passions manifest in the world. When life is feeling cloudy and dull, call on Honeybee to help you navigate toward joy. During dark times, she reminds you that clouds pass and your passion and purpose will be revealed again.

Ritual

FOLLOW THE SUN

Honeybee is a creature of sunlight and reminds us of the importance of following the sun, feeling into its rhythm, and remembering the cycle of the seasons.

As we move between the solstices, the angle of the sun changes. Honeybee knows this instinctively. Dedicate some time to following the sun to get yourself more deeply aligned with your inner compass.

Note where on the horizon the sun rises and where it sets. This is a beautiful way to begin and end your days, reminding yourself that you too are a child of the sun and the earth.

If you're able, add a midday moment with the sun. Without looking directly at it, notice how high it is in the sky. You can use a tree as a measuring rod, noting how high or low the sun sits at various times of year.

If you track your observations in your calendar or date book, you'll begin to understand the cycles and rhythms of the sun's motions.

> *Far away there in the sunshine are my highest aspirations. I may not reach them, but I can look up and see their beauty, believe in them, and try to follow where they lead.*
>
> Louisa May Alcott

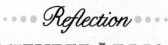

HONEYBEE LESSONS

Two and a half million years ago, our ancestors' brains suddenly grew exponentially. The human brain uses an incredible amount of glucose, which honey, as a food source, provides. Some say Honeybee was a key player in our own evolution. Isn't it interesting that it's our big brains that cause us to overanalyze and ruminate — two of the things most likely to put out our fire and dampen our passion.

Do you overthink things and put out your inner flame?

Honeybee creates a surplus of honey (her own liquid sunshine) to get her and her hive through the winter months.

How can you, like Honeybee, store some of life's liquid gold so you have a little sunshine when you need it?

Made of interlocking hexagons that bees build cooperatively and efficiently, a beehive is a highly organized place! There is a nursery for the little ones, and rooms where worker bees pack pollen and nectar into cells then cap the cells with wax.

Where does your life need a little extra organization?

Know Your Song
HOUSE FINCH

Haemorhous mexicanus

House Finch's song is so sunny and sweet that in the 1940s a speculator tried to sell this small bird as a pet, which he called the Hollywood Finch (a reference to the finch's West Coast roots). The ploy was a flop, perhaps because House Finch can't compete with Parrot for beauty and cage appeal. Unable to sell his stash of songbirds, the speculator released House Finch and friends on Long Island, and from there they quickly spread to bird feeders across the United States. If you, like Finch, have ever been deemed "not enough," remember, this is exactly how House Finch escaped his gilded cage. Despite being judged as "not enough," Finch still sings like a star. You too have a strength, a song. Do you know what it is?

WHAT THOUGHTS KEEP YOU FROM FLYING?

Sometimes we get trapped by our own desires or by other people's expectations. It's time to uncage yourself.

Grab your journal and find a quiet place to sit. Take a few deep breaths to center and calm yourself, then make a list of thoughts, expectations, or desires (yours or someone else's) that make you feel trapped. Your sentences might start like this:

A good daughter always...

I should...

It's important to...

My grandma (mother, father, boss) will be disappointed if...

Choose one and ask yourself: *If this thought was located in my body, where would it live?*

Don't overthink this! Your first answer is the answer. After you've located the thought in your body, imagine disengaging it. You might envision cutting the cord between yourself and the thought, or digging it out and tossing it in the compost.

One by one, visualize disengaging from each entrapping thought. You may need to do this a few times to make it stick in your psyche.

····· *Reflection* ·····
THE FLIP SIDE OF WISHES

House Finch can thank his plain and tatty feathers for giving him the freedom to fly. If he had been a more beautiful bird — if his looks had matched his singing voice — he'd be known as the Hollywood Finch and be living in a cage.

While "house" may be a less glamorous moniker than "Hollywood," Finch is here to remind you that "having it all" isn't always what it seems to be.

In our desire to be *more* — more beautiful, richer, more charismatic — we rarely stop to think about the flip side of those seemingly desirous traits: being super smart can be super lonely; having a gorgeous body might mean people judge you before they know you; being really rich leaves you open to jealousy.

Instead of focusing on how perfect life would be if only you were _____ (fill in the blank with your recurring wish!), think about a gift you already have, like House Finch's song, that you could amplify and share.

You Are Worthy

TABBY CAT

Felis catus

Twitching in the sunlight, Tabby Cat has ancestral dreams of savannahs and sleeping in rocky crevices. A descendant of the wild ones, Tabby still bears the remnants of her stripes and spots. But she's pleased to have moved indoors. *Adopting humans was a brilliant move*, she purrs, stretching and kneading her paws. Tabby never wonders if she's *earned* the warm patch of sunlight by the window or the bit of tuna in her evening meal. She never doubts that she is worthy. Tabby licks a paw to smooth the fur behind her ear. *You are already enough*, she reminds you. Breathe into that knowing.

····•• *Ritual* ••····
BATHE YOUR ENERGY

In Ancient Egypt, Cat was a representative of the Goddess Bast come to dwell in your home. She was family royalty. When a cat died, she was mummified, and her humans shaved their eyebrows and mourned her until their eyebrows grew back.

In ancient Celtic lands, Druids used Cat medicine to help them slip between the worlds. During the Spanish Inquisition, cats were seen as familiars — magical avatars who assisted with sorcery. Cat is associated with divinity and magic because she keeps her energy attuned. You can keep your own energy field clear with regular cat baths:

- Close your eyes and take a few deep breaths, letting yourself settle into your skin.
- Using your hands, begin smoothing down your energy field, a few inches out from your physical body. Not sure you believe that you have an energy field? That's okay! Go through the motions and notice what you feel.
- If you notice any spot that feels sticky or rough, pluck it out of your energy field and flick it away. Trust your hands and don't overthink it.

Cat knows that keeping your energy field clean is an important step in cultivating a magical glow.

Reflection
DEPENDENCE AND INDEPENDENCE

Some say that domesticated cats, compared to their ancestors, are forever in the kitten stage, never learning to hunt or take care of themselves. Humans have become their surrogate mothers, taking care of all their needs. But Tabby Cat's aura of self-sufficiency and independence seems at odds with this notion.

Is it possible to be both independent and reliant on others?

Can you be fully content with life while not in complete control?

Mountain Lion is the wild and full-grown cousin of Cat. Mountain Lion takes Tabby Cat's teachings up a notch, helping us grasp not only our own worth but the worth of others; to watch and observe in order to come to understanding; and to move through the world balancing power with intentional action. Mountain Lion leads herself and doesn't worry about who follows (and ironically, because of this, sometimes she ends up with a trail of initiates).

Delight in Daring
FIVE-LINED SKINK

Plestiodon fasciatus

Five-lined Skink is an adrenaline junkie, the Evel Knievel of the lizard world. This speed demon flashes his bright blue tail, baiting hawks and snakes. *Catch me if you can!* Skink trills, diving into a crevice. Skink knows he's superfast, but that's not why he baits the big boys. His superpower is beyond speed: Skink can lose his tail and live. So he flicks it around like a bright blue flag and then scurries for the shadows, cackling as he goes. Skink reminds you to delight in daring, that to really live you have to be willing to risk your tail.

···· *Ritual* ····

RELEASE REGRET

Twenty years from now you will probably be more disappointed by the things you didn't do than by the things you did.

Looking back on your life, what have you left undone?
What regrets do you have for missed opportunities?

Whether it's a trip you didn't take, a job you turned down, or a friend you didn't make time for, understanding your regrets helps you to make different choices moving forward.

So, list your regrets. Go back year by year. Use the calendar so you can be precise.

Once you have a list, take it one step further: Sit with each regret and ask if you still have sadness or grief around this moment. If you don't, if you feel complete, let it go.

But if there's still an emotional pull, take time to understand why. Was it a missed opportunity for personal growth? Was it a crossroads in your life where you feel like you chose the wrong road?

Understanding your regrets helps you understand your own choices and allows you to make different ones in the future.

GROWING THROUGH LOSS

Regret is often linked to the times you didn't dare, the opportunities you missed because you were too scared of what you might lose or have to give up.

Skink knows that when he loses his tail a new one will grow in its place.

This is one of life's great secrets: When you lose something, you are inadvertently creating room for something new to grow.

You've probably already experienced this in your own life. Think about the things you've lost: people, jobs, homes . . .

Loss breaks your heart. But it also shows you your strength, and that's where the growth comes in.

What have you learned about yourself through loss?

What new growth has come because you've lost your metaphoric tail?

When your cup is empty, you do not mourn what is gone. Because if you do, you will miss the opportunity to fill it again.

Sarah Addison Allen,
Lost Lake

Key In to Wisdom
LITTLE OWL

Athene noctua

Little Owl has been the companion of a Goddess and the patron of a city, so don't let the word "little" fool you. This icon of wisdom sat on the Athena's blind side, illuminating what even a Goddess could not see. Athena, Greek Goddess of Wisdom, knew that being wise requires us to acknowledge our own weaknesses, to understand that even Goddesses are not all-knowing. Blindness in and of itself is not a fault; failure comes from refusing to call on those who will help you understand the whole. Little Owl sees what you cannot. Call on her when you're ready to listen.

····•·· *Ritual* ··•····

ASK WISE QUESTIONS

Little Owl teaches us that even a Goddess can't know and see everything. Each of us has a blind side created by enculturation, prejudice, or simple lack of understanding.

Of course, it's hard to know what you don't know.

When facing decisions where you need to see the biggest possible picture, it's helpful to have some ritual questions to ask yourself. You can even deputize a close friend to ask you these questions when you come looking for advice:

- How will this situation look in five years? Or a decade from now?

- What will the outcome of my decisions look like in five years? A decade?

- Am I attached to being right?

- Are there parts of myself that I will lose if I behave a certain way?

- What decision might create the highest good for all involved?

···· *Reflection* ····
CALLING IN COUNSEL

It takes a bit of bravery and a lot of self-awareness to admit you have a blind side, that you are not all knowing... especially if you're a Goddess!

If Little Owl were to sit on your shoulder, what types of things would she need to whisper to you? What areas of your life sit in your personal blind spot?

Can you admit when you're wrong?

Do you allow people around you to change, or do you insist on seeing them in a fixed way?

Are you too trusting or not trusting enough?

Do you have trouble with money? Or business? Or science?

Are you willfully ignorant of how other people feel about you?

Acknowledging areas in your life where you are blind allows you to strategize and call in the support you need, whether that's an accountant or a therapist. You can think of these helpers as your own Little Owls and know that when you allow yourself counsel and advice, you are moving toward wisdom.

Shape-Shift
RED FOX

Vulpes vulpes

Despite being a redhead, Fox understands the subtleties of camouflage. One moment she seems to be a small dog, the next a log, and then she'll move gracefully as a cat. In Asia, she's been seen wearing the face of a beautiful woman and sometimes of an old man. Fox is said to gain a tail as she masters her magic; a fox with nine tails knows many things including invisibility and the art of shape-shifting. Fox is a starlet-turned-spy, ready to stand out or blend in . . . and having the wisdom to know which is needed. Fox teaches that your exterior is an ever-changeable illusion. If she has appeared, see if it's time for a shift, or if, perhaps, someone is being shifty with you!

···• *Ritual* •···

ENERGETIC CAMOUFLAGE

Fox is at home slinking down a suburban street or running in the cornfields. She easily shape-shifts her exterior to blend into her environment. You can, too.

Energy follows intention. So begin reworking your energy signature by thinking about what's making you stand out from the background energetic pattern. Are you moving too fast or too slow? Are you being too loud or too quiet? Are you projecting meekness or confidence?

To energetically camouflage yourself, you need to vibrate at the same frequency as the world around you, aligning energetically with your surroundings. Shape-shifting begins with changing your energy. Then you'll change the way you move your body to align with that new energy.

Focus on the energy you're projecting and shift it with intention. If you're moving too fast, consciously decide to slow down. If you're being too meek, consciously decide to project confidence. This simple shift begins your energetic camouflage.

Deepen the illusion by feeling into the energy you've donned and letting your body move in sync with it.

Play with energetic camouflage when you don't need it, so you've mastered this ritual for the times when you do.

··•• *Reflection* ••··
THE NEED TO BE SEEN

Fox has no ego attachment to being seen. She's perfectly happy to slink through the shadows and be mistaken for a dog or deer.

Do you have attachment to being seen?
To being known just as you are?

Have you demanded others see you as you see yourself?

Oftentimes we differentiate ourselves from others, especially our family, by highlighting our differences. Like Fox's look-at-me red coat, this is one side of Fox's medicine coin. The other side is the ability to blend, to not be seen, to become invisible.

She spent an astonishing amount of time in attending lectures and demonstrations . . . and such-like activities. It paid, she said; it was camouflage. If you kept the small rules you could break the big ones.

George Orwell, 1984

Can you embrace both sides
of this medicine and be both
the starlet and the spy?

Commune with Nature

BLUE DAMSELFLY

Enallagma cyathigerum

Damselfly is a creature of water and sunlight, her rainbow wings moving faster than the human eye can follow. Only partially of this mortal realm, Damselfly can lead you to the interstitial spaces where magic lives and the earth elementals dance, showing you the rich complexity that exists in even the smallest patch of the natural world. Look to these tiny beings to be seduced, so you can fall in love again with the wonder of life and being alive. When you release the illusions woven by culture and civilization, you'll find your own effervescence and iridescence. *What's real?* Blue Damselfly asks. *And what do you want to be real?*

·····Ritual·····
TEND THE MAGIC

Nature exudes its own magic. When we tend to it, we begin to recognize magic within ourselves. Set the intention to tend to the natural world and feed the forces you cannot see:

- Put out offerings for the elementals. These ephemeral energies live alongside us and play in the natural places (some people call them fairies). In Ireland, traditional offerings were milk, honey, and whiskey. In the Americas, native peoples offered cornmeal and tobacco. Other offerings can include a song, a prayer, or Reiki.

- Build a cairn in your yard. These stacks of stones are a way to pause and honor the natural world. They're a prayer made physical.

- Plant a garden.

- Bring home a potted plant.

- Hang wind chimes.

- Keep a bird bath in your garden, yard, or on your deck.

- Put prisms and mirrors in the garden.

- Sing to the birds.

- Build a bee hotel for the carpenter bees.

Whatever you choose to do, do it in the spirit of reverence and intentional connection.

Reflection · · · ·
RECOGNIZING SMALL MAGICS

Are you always looking for big magic and ignoring the small, every-day magics that make life beautiful?

Life is full of serendipitous and magical moments, like when you get a call from a friend just as you're dialing her number, or when you ask for a "sign" and find a feather on your morning walk. These moments fade into the background unless you actively acknowledge them. Sometimes, in our desire for big magic — the lightning bolt or fireworks — we forget these small moments that warm our lives like candle glow.

Do you recognize and nurture the
small magics in your life?

Dragonfly may get all the glory but when it comes to iridescence it is cousin Damselfly who truly sparkles! These critters are quite similar, but for the set of their wings, and are often thought of interchangeably.

153

Slide into Joy
RIVER OTTER

Lontra canadensis

This fashionista of the waterways stays warm in her plush
fur coat, and by wriggling and squiggling, generating heat
with her ridiculously high metabolism. River Otter's inner
fire is fueled by constant snacking on crayfish and crabs. The
cynical might say she's joyful because she gets to eat all day
and not gain an ounce.

But River Otter knows that when you're lit from within, life
provides endless amusement. *Take that muddy riverbank for
instance,* River Otter says. *I see a waterslide. Do you see it?*
River Otter reminds you to actively look for joy. She knows
it's there, waiting to be found.

···· *Ritual* ····

HAPPINESS PAST AND PRESENT

Human brains are wired for survival, for noticing the obstacle in our path so we can find our way around it. Which means we often remember the rough stuff but have to work more conscientiously to remember the good.

You might be surprised at how much joy you've experienced in the past year. The trick is to begin to recognize it.

List at least 30 happy moments that you are grateful for. Use your calendar to go month by month, remembering and noting achievements, reunions, lunches with friends — anything that made you smile.

You're training your mind to recognize joy . . . and you might be surprised by how much you've had!

Gratitude shifts your perspective from lack to abundance and allows you to focus on the good in your life.

Jen Sincero

To continue noticing joy in your daily life, keep a gratitude journal. Each evening, note at least two things that brought you joy over the course of the day. You don't have to create an entire journal entry, just choose a few words to remind you of your own happiness.

WHAT'S YOUR ENERGY SPECTRUM?

Sea Otter is cousin to River Otter, but her energy is different. While River Otter is in constant motion, Sea Otter's motions are more leisurely. She spends a lot of time floating on her back. She'll groom her pup in this position, crack open mussels with a rock she keeps in a pouch under her arm, soak up a bit of sunshine, and even sleep (holding paws with other Sea Otters so they don't get separated – yes, it's simply adorable).

River Otter and Sea Otter are joyful critters. Their differences teach us that any given energy has a full spectrum of expression. Sea Otter expresses contented joy while River Otter has a more electric way of being. Sea Otter tends to conserve energy while River Otter spends it with abandon.

All emotions and actions exist on a spectrum.

What spectrums are you working with in your life? Are you cruising from anger to elation? Are you dealing in shades of contentment or discontent? Do you swing from jealousy to generosity?

Understanding the spectrum helps you see your daily actions and emotions in the larger context of your life and helps you gain the perspective to resolve them.

Remember Forgetting

HUMAN

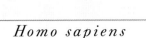

Homo sapiens

Someday, when the animals gather to tell the tales of being, they will say, *Remember when humans went through the Great Forgetting? They forgot they were one of us. They forgot we are brothers and sisters. They forgot they, too, are of the earth.* The animals will shake their heads and ruffle their feathers remembering the rift and near catastrophic destruction the humans caused in the throes of their forgetting.

Even now, humans know there is something missing, something lost. We live our lives with a nagging nostalgia, a longing for something we can't quite name.

What is it that you are forgetting?

···· *Ritual* ····
CREATE A COUNCIL

Humans tend to be *Homo sapiens*-centric, looking at the world primarily through the lens of human need. What happens if you widen your point of view?

Choose three animal spirits as your council of advisors. These could be animals with whom you already feel a kinship, or you could select them by using the cards that come with this book.

Now, use free writing to channel each animal's perspective:

Grab your notebook or journal.

Set a timer for 10 minutes.

Begin with this prompt: *This is* [animal advisor]. *While you humans are ingenious and creative, you don't always see the big picture. Here's what you are missing...*

Start writing and don't stop until the timer goes off. You'll probably feel silly or lost for the first few minutes. You may even feel like you're just making things up. That's okay. It takes a little time to sink into the flow. Keep writing! At a certain point your ego will step aside and let the magic happen.

Do this with each of your animals, and return to this technique when you need advice and guidance.

WHAT MAKES US HUMAN?

Over the centuries many great thinkers have written about what
defines a human:

Is it that we use tools?

That we create language?

Is it our ability to debate philosophy and morality?

*Are humans defined by our
ingenuity, or our destructiveness?*

Is the ability to love a defining human trait?

What makes humans human?

*In the Western tradition there is a
recognized hierarchy of beings, with,
of course, the human being on top –
the pinnacle of evolution, the darling
of Creation – and the plants at the
bottom. But in Native ways of knowing,
human people are often referred to as
"the younger brothers" of Creation.*

Robin Wall Kimmerer,
Braiding Sweetgrass

How to Work with the Bestiary Cards

When you first open your cards, spend a few minutes getting acquainted. Allow your eyes and your mind to wander as you look at the pictures.

If you're familiar with smudging, use sage, palo santo, cedar, or sweetgrass to clear your cards and set an intention for their use. Think of it as the beginning of a relationship; open your heart and introduce yourself.

As you read through the Bestiary, you'll notice each animal holds a spectrum of energy. For instance, Cat speaks to us of self-worth. You may or may not have a sense of your own worth, so how you think about yourself has implications for how you will read the card. Pulling the Cat card tells you to focus on your self-worth, and you may then find it's out of balance in one way or another or that you're coming into a time period when your sense of self-worth will be challenged. Always keep in mind the full range of each animal's medicine.

ONE-CARD DRAW

The simplest way to use your deck is to focus your mind on a particular topic or conundrum in your life and hold this thought as you shuffle the deck. When you feel ready, pick a card. While some people say to draw a card off the top of the deck, I think it's just as useful to fan the cards and pull whichever you're drawn to.

You can also simply use a soft gaze to study the pictures, drawing the animal that feels intuitively right for you to work with in this moment.

Drawing a card cracks open the door to the collective unconscious — the world of meanings and symbols — where you can gain a new way of approaching aspects of your personality or thinking about circumstances in your life. I find it far more useful to think of the cards as *illuminating* (which gives you free will and room to pivot on your path) than *prophesizing* (which denies your ability to create many possible futures). And remember, these cards are merely a tool to help you tap in. Your own insights are as valuable as mine, so let your intuition sing!

TWO CARDS: THE CROSSING

A different way to approach the cards is to choose one card to represent you and then draw a card to see what's crossing you.

The card that crosses you gives you insight into places where you might be stuck, or perhaps it will bring clarity to a situation that you're not seeing clearly. It also might indicate where your thinking might be false or the story you're telling yourself needs to shift.

CALLING IN GUIDANCE

Animal Spirit medicine can be called in for guidance on a particular situation or more broadly to guide you through a period of your life.

Draw a card with your left hand.

Now draw a card with your right.

The animal on your left is showing up to guide your inward journey. This might include emotional explorations, dreamwork, and journeywork. You can ask this animal to meet you in the dreamtime or during a shamanic journey to serve as a guide.

The animal on your right is showing up to guide your outward work: how you move through the physical world. This may include how you behave in your relationships with others, your work (whether for pay or not), travel, how you care for your family, and how you tend to your spaces. Call on this animal to serve as a guide as you go about your everyday life.

These animals are committing their support to you. What will you commit in return? This commitment might be expressed internally – a thank-you before bed each night, for instance – or externally. External expressions of gratitude might be an altar you tend, or donating to a charity that supports your animal in the physical world.

Remember, each reading reflects what you need to know in the present moment. Change is constant – there is not one reading that lasts forever. Instead, use your cards to have an ongoing dialogue and deepening of your relationship with yourself and the world around you.

And sometimes a cigar is just a cigar . . .

A black cat crossing your path signifies that the animal is going somewhere.
Groucho Marx

SOURCES & RESOURCES

In writing this book, I've read up on folklore and legend; listened to hoots and growls and underwater songs; watched countless videos (with the sound turned off!); and researched animal biology. Deep bows to the following organizations for the thorough and readable information on their websites: The Cornell Lab of Ornithology, National Audubon Society, National Geographic, and Smithsonian.

The first animal medicine book I bought for myself was Jessica Dawn Palmer's *Animal Wisdom: The Definitive Guide to the Myth, Folklore and Medicine Power of Animals.* I still hurry home to this book when a hawk crosses my path or when the bears reappear in early spring.

I recently bought *Medicine Cards: The Discovery of Power Through the Ways of Animals* by Jamie Sams and David Carson. After a crazy Mountain Lion sighting, it was this book that made sense of this new-to-me energy.

Thank-Yous

This book had been on my heart and shimmering in my subconscious for over a year when my publishing house said, "Let's do it *now*!" Huge thank-yous to everyone at Storey Publishing and to the inimitable Kate O'Hara who pulled together to make this happen: Deborah, Liz, Jessica, Alee, and everyone working behind the scenes whose guidance and care for my books is so appreciated.

Big thanks to my agent Laura Lee Mattingly at Present Perfect Dept. for suggesting the ferry, doing the details, and being a sounding board. I'm already eyeing-up lunch spots for my next visit to San Francisco!

Deepest bows to Shannon Thayer for expertly grabbing the reins when I unexpectedly announced I was writing another book . . . *right now*. Thank you, Shan, this one couldn't have been hatched without you (and, sorry, no Turkey entry here!).

Writing this book could have devolved into a stay-in-my-pajamas-write-and-eat-gluten-free-frozen-pizza frenzy but my friends made sure I got clean air and fresh food. Big love, beauties. You all make my every day so much more magical. And Marianne, thanks for the reliquary and the necessary refueling.

To my Medicine Keepers and Witch Campers, for doing this walk with me. And double thanks to those of you who had Kim Krans's Wild Unknown Animal Spirit deck delivered to my door the day I finished this manuscript ('cause I wouldn't let myself look at it before then!).

Mom and Dad, you'll always have my thanks for years of horses . . . even when (especially when) it made no sense.

And a Bestiary wouldn't be complete without mention of my best beasties, Nyssa and Finn, for making me laugh, keeping me sane, and making sure I never lack for balls, ducks, and roosters. And always, to Andrew, not least of all for letting me sleep in during the morning beast walk. XO.

Discover the

WILD WISDOM OF PLANTS

with Maia Toll's first book

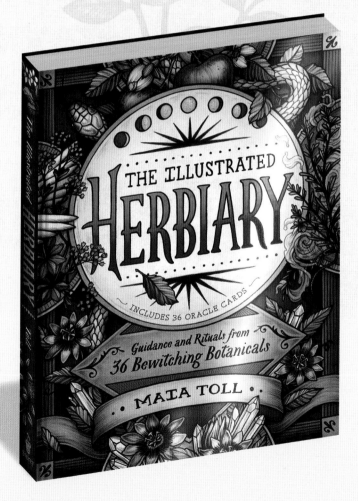

MAIA TOLL

Family myth insists that the first word out of Maia's mouth was "horsey." It's a good story, and a fabulous setup for a life focused on connection with the spirit and energy of the natural world. Maia trained with a medicine woman in Ireland, learning healing craft by working with both humans and animals on an organic farm. She has taught botanical medicine at universities, hospitals, and even in the Peruvian jungle. In 2005, Maia opened a tiny herbal apothecary in Philadelphia, which has since grown into Herbiary, a multi-city natural wellness and sacred living store that she runs with her husband, Andrew. Maia's first book, *The Illustrated Herbiary*, was published in 2018. When not obsessively reading, "talking" to stones, or drinking copious amounts of tea, Maia teaches and blogs to an international following at maiatoll.com, where she helps women cultivate a sense of deep connection, spiritual strength, and inner-knowing.